THE
COCKER
SPANIEL

by Charlotte Wilcox

Content Consultant
Louise A. Milner
President
The American Spaniel Club, Inc.

C A P S T O N E   P R E S S
M A N K A T O ,   M I N N E S O T A

C A P S T O N E P R E S S
818 North Willow Street • Mankato, MN 56001
http://www.capstone-press.com

Printed in the United States of America.

Library of Congress Cataloging-in-Publication Data
Wilcox, Charlotte.
　　The cocker spaniel/by Charlotte Wilcox.
　　p. cm.--(Learning about dogs)
　　Includes bibliographical references and index.
　　Summary: An introduction to this friendly and popular dog, which includes its history, development, uses, and care.
　　ISBN 1-56065-540-2
　　1. Cocker spaniels--Juvenile literature. [1. Cocker spaniels. 2. Dogs.]
I. Title. II. Series: Wilcox, Charlotte. Learning about dogs.
SF429.C55W55 1998
636.752'4--dc21

　　　　　　　　　　　　　　　　　97-12207
　　　　　　　　　　　　　　　　　CIP
　　　　　　　　　　　　　　　　　AC

Photo credits
Reynolds Photography, cover, 12, 14, 22, 24
Jack MacFarlane, 4, 10, 28, 34
Unicorn Stock/Karen Holsinger Mullen, 6; Tom McCarthy,
　　16, 32; Kathi Corder, 26; Martha McBride, 31
Faith A. Uridel, 9, 37, 38
Betty Crowell, 18
Index Stock, 21
Visuals Unlimited/Carolyn Galati, 40-41

Table of Contents

Quick Facts about the Cocker Spaniel

Description

Height:

Male cocker spaniels stand 14-1/2 to 15-1/2 inches (37 to 39 centimeters) tall. Females stand 13-1/2 to 14-1/2 inches (34-37 centimeters) tall. Height is measured from the ground to the withers. The withers are the tops of the shoulders.

Weight:

Cocker spaniels weigh 22 to 28 pounds (10 to 13 kilograms).

Physical features: Cocker spaniels are small to medium in size. They have long, furry ears. Their legs and feet also have extra fur. Cockers have large, brown eyes. Their tails are usually cut short.

Color: Cockers come in many colors. They can be solid black, brown, cream, tan, or reddish brown. They can also be a combination of these colors and white. Some may have tan markings.

Development

Place of origin: Cocker spaniels were developed in England.

History of breed: Cocker spaniels came from hunting dogs of Spain.

Numbers: About 50,000 cocker spaniels are registered every year in the United States. Register means to record a dog's breeding records with an official club. About 2,000 cocker spaniels are registered each year in Canada. Many more are born but are not registered.

Uses

Most cocker spaniels in North America are family pets. A few cocker spaniels still hunt with their owners.

Chapter 1

The Happy Spaniel

Some people say cocker spaniels are one of the happiest dog breeds. A cocker will be happy in almost any home as long as it receives plenty of attention. Cockers need to be with people, and they love children. Most dogs wag their tails when they are happy. Cocker spaniels do more than that. Sometimes they wag their whole hind quarters.

Cocker spaniels love being part of a family. They also like to be a part of family activities. Cocker spaniels enjoy being outside. They are active dogs, but they are obedient and gentle. They often show affection by licking people. Cocker spaniels need human companionship. They are very loyal to their families.

Cockers need to be with people, and they love children.

Cockers are popular because of their pleasing personalities. But they are also popular because they are so handsome. They have silky coats that come in many colors.

A Big Hit

Lady and the Tramp was a hit Disney movie in the 1950s. It was the story of two dogs. Tramp was a street mongrel. A mongrel is a dog of mixed breeding. Lady was a beautiful cocker spaniel. She helped make the movie so popular. But cocker spaniels were a big hit long before the movie came out.

Cocker spaniels have been a favorite in North America for most of the 20th century. They were the number one dog from the 1930s to the 1980s.

Cocker spaniels have pleasing personalities and handsome, silky coats.

Chapter 2

The Beginnings
of the Breed

Cockers are part of the spaniel family of dogs. All spaniels have long ears. They have silky coats. They have extra-long hair on their ears and legs. This hair is called feathering.

Today, there are several breeds of spaniels. Some spaniel breeds are larger than others. The cocker is the smallest spaniel breed.

All spaniels are hunting dogs by nature. Some modern spaniel breeds are still hunting dogs. But cocker spaniels do not hunt much anymore. Most of them are pets.

Cockers have extra-long hair on their ears.

Cockers are good hunters. They wag their tails when they smell an animal or a bird.

Beginnings in Spain

Breeders believe spaniels came from Spain. The word spaniel means someone from Spain. Spanish hunters used dogs to help them hunt hundreds of years ago.

Smaller hound breeds developed a keen sense of smell. They hunted mostly by scent. Hunters trained the dogs to sneak up on game. Game is wild animals or birds that are hunted. The dogs would sneak up on one side. The hunter would sneak up on the other side.

The dog could smell where the game was hiding. When the dog caught the scent of an animal or bird, it wagged its tail. The minute the hunter saw his dog's tail wag, he moved toward the game. At that moment, the dog would spring at the game from the other side.

They chased the game into the hunters' nets. They also chased game out of places hunters could not reach. Some hounds were trained to kill the game and bring it to the hunter.

For this type of hunting, small dogs were best. Small dogs could get closer to the game without being seen.

Spaniels Come to England

Spaniels came to England more than 600 years ago. King Henry VIII ruled England in the

Some spaniels are black and white.

1500s. He had many types of hunting dogs.
Henry VIII had a special servant named Robin.
Robin's title was the King's Spaniel Keeper.
His job was to take care of the royal spaniels.

At first, all spaniels in England were
considered one breed. But they were of many
different sizes. The largest weighed up to 70

pounds (31 kilograms). The smallest weighed as little as 10 pounds (4.5 kilograms). Different-sized dogs sometimes came from the same litter. A litter is a family of puppies born at one time.

Larger spaniels were called springer spaniels. They earned this name because they were good at springing upon game at just the right moment. Springer spaniels are still popular hunting dogs in North America and Europe.

The smaller spaniels came to be known as cocker spaniels. They earned their name because they often hunted a game bird called the woodcock.

BAMBI

Chapter 3

The Development of the Breed

Today, cocker spaniels are well-known. Champion cockers can win trophies at dog shows. But cockers were not even considered a separate breed until 1892. The first cocker to be registered with the Kennel Club of England was named Captain. He was registered as a spaniel in 1878.

One very famous cocker spaniel was born in England in 1879. His name was Obo. His father was a Sussex spaniel. His mother was a field spaniel. Obo was considered a cocker because he was small. Obo was used to start the cocker line in North America.

Champion cocker spaniels can win trophies at dog shows.

Almost all cockers in North America came from the four sons of Robinhurst Foreglow.

Cockers in North America

Obo was bred to a female cocker spaniel. This female was moved to Canada. She gave birth to Obo's puppies there. The best one was a small male. He had a curly black coat. He had a lot of feathering on his legs.

The little black cocker was named Obo II. A dog breeder from New Hampshire bought him. Obo II had a grandson named Robinhurst Foreglow. This dog had four famous sons.

Red Brucie, Sandspring Surmise, and Midcliff Miracle Man were champion cockers in the United States. Limestone Laddie was a champion in Canada. These dogs were handsome. They also had good personalities.

Soon, everyone wanted a puppy from Robinhurst Foreglow's line. Almost all cocker spaniels in North America today came from those four sons of Robinhurst Foreglow.

Two Cocker Breeds

In 1881, breeders from the United States and Canada met together. They formed the American Spaniel Club.

Some people who belonged to this club had cockers from Robinhurst Foreglow's line. These dogs were the North American line. Other people had cockers from English lines.

But the English and American cockers were different. American cocker spaniels were bred mostly to be pets. They were smaller than their English cousins. Their coats were longer and softer. Most North Americans liked the prettier American cockers.

A few people still wanted a cocker spaniel that could hunt. They preferred the English type. But there were fewer and fewer English puppies around. Hunters feared that the owners of English cockers would breed their dogs with American cockers. If that happened, there might not be any cockers left that were good hunters.

In 1935, some breeders formed the English Cocker Spaniel Club of America. They wanted to make sure the English lines stayed pure. In 1946, the American Kennel Club named the English cocker spaniel a separate breed.

Numbers of Cockers

The American cocker spaniel remains one of North America's favorite breeds. In the 1980s, yearly registrations reached nearly 100,000. Now about 50,000 are registered every year in the United States. About 2,000 are registered each year in Canada.

There are more American cocker spaniels than English cocker spaniels. Fewer than 1,500 English cocker spaniels are registered in North America each year.

The cocker spaniel is one of the most popular breeds in the United States and Canada.

Chapter 4

The Cocker Spaniel Today

Cocker spaniels are best known for their beauty. They have brown eyes and almost always look happy. People also love their personalities. Cockers are very loving.

What Cocker Spaniels Look Like

Cocker spaniels are small to medium in size. The height of a dog is measured from the ground to the withers. The withers are the tops of the shoulders. Male cocker spaniels stand 14-1/2 to 15-1/2 inches (37 to 39 centimeters) tall. Females stand 13-1/2 to 14-1/2 inches (34 to 37 centimeters) tall. Cockers can weigh from 22 to 28 pounds (10 to 13 kilograms).

Cocker spaniels are best known for their beauty.

Like all spaniel breeds, cockers have medium to long coats. Their coats are soft, shiny, and silky. They have fluffy feathering on their ears and lower bodies. The feathering bounces when they move.

Cocker spaniels come in many colors. They can be solid black, brown, cream, tan, or reddish brown. They can also be a combination of these colors and white. Some have tan markings. Cockers can also be roan. Roan is white mixed in with a darker color.

Cockers have coats that are soft, silky, and shiny.

Chapter 5

Owning a Cocker Spaniel

Cocker spaniels make great pets. They do not need a lot of room or special equipment. They are a good choice for people who have never owned a dog before. They get along well with small children. In fact, they get along well with almost everyone.

But cocker spaniels may not be right for people with allergies. An allergy is a sickness or a skin reaction caused by contact with something. Cockers shed more hair than short-haired breeds. They may leave hair on furniture and carpets. People with allergies may react to the dog hair.

Cocker spaniels get along well with almost everyone.

Looking for a Cocker Spaniel

A pet store is not always the best place to find a cocker spaniel. Some puppies sold in pet stores are bred in puppy mills. These are places where dogs are bred just to sell. The breeders often do not care about good qualities.

Many dogs raised in puppy mills have health problems. They may also have personality problems. This is because they do not receive human affection when they are young.

Most pet buyers are not able to spot these problems. It is safer to buy a puppy from a good breeder. The American Kennel Club or the American Spaniel Club can suggest a good local breeder. A registered cocker spaniel puppy may cost more than $200.

It is important to select a healthy puppy.

Adult dogs may be found at a nearby rescue shelter. Rescue shelters find homes for abandoned dogs. These dogs cost less than one from a breeder. Some rescued dogs are even free. Many are already trained.

Bringing A Cocker Home

Cocker spaniels need a special place all their own. A basket, a dog bed, or a crate works well. The bed should have a soft surface, such as an old blanket or pillow. It should be in a quiet place. It should be away from drafts or direct heat.

A cocker spaniel needs a fenced in place to run. This will keep the cocker in its own yard. It will also keep other animals out. Larger dogs can injure or even kill a cocker spaniel. Stray dogs may carry sicknesses.

It is important to be able to find a cocker if it gets lost. It should have its owner's name and phone number on its collar. Or it can have a microchip implanted under its skin. A microchip is a computer chip about the size of a grain of rice. When scanned, it reveals the owner's name, address, and telephone number.

Cocker spaniels make great pets.

Feeding

Cocker spaniels need peace and quiet when they are eating. A dog should not be disturbed while it is eating. Cockers usually eat and drink from narrow bowls. This helps them keep their long ears out of the food and water.

The best diet is good-quality dog food. It comes dry or canned. How much the dog needs depends on its size and age. A full-grown cocker spaniel may eat half a pound (228 grams) or more of dog food each day. Or it may eat one can of canned food.

Many dogs eat all their food in one meal. Some owners divide the food into two meals. A dog should not be fed more than it needs. It is not healthy for a dog to be overweight.

Dogs need plenty of clean water all the time. Otherwise, a dog needs a chance to drink at least three times a day.

Cockers need healthy food every day. Every now and then they enjoy a snack.

Grooming

The cocker's long hair picks up dirt and mud. It also gets tangled. Cocker spaniels need to be brushed every two or three days. When they are shedding, they should be brushed every day.

If a cocker gets dirty, brushing may not be enough. It will need a bath. It is best to use a gentle shampoo or a shampoo made just for dogs. All the shampoo must be rinsed out. Then the dog should be dried with a towel or a hair dryer.

A cocker's nails should be trimmed if they get too long. Once a week, its teeth should be cleaned with baking soda or dog toothpaste.

The cocker spaniel's long ears also need care. Ears must be kept very clean. A veterinarian can give advice about how to do these things. A veterinarian is a person trained and qualified to treat the sicknesses and injuries of animals.

Cocker spaniels need to be brushed often.

Health Care

Dogs need shots every year to protect them from serious illnesses. They need pills to protect them from heartworms. A heartworm is a tiny worm carried by mosquitoes that enters a dog's heart and slowly destroys it. Dogs need checkups every year for all types of worms.

During warm weather, a cocker should be checked every day for ticks. A tick is a small bug that sucks blood. Some ticks carry Lyme disease. Lyme disease is a serious illness that can cripple an animal or a human. A dog must be checked often for fleas, lice, and mites. These are tiny insects that live on a dog's skin.

During warm weather, a cocker must be checked every day for ticks.

Exercise and Love

Cocker spaniels may be small, but they are active. They need opportunities to run or walk often. Cockers can roam freely in a fenced yard. Otherwise they will need to be taken for walks.

Cocker spaniels thrive on good care, a proper diet, and plenty of exercise. Given love and attention, they will be a family's best friend for many years.

Cocker spaniels can roam freely in a fenced yard.

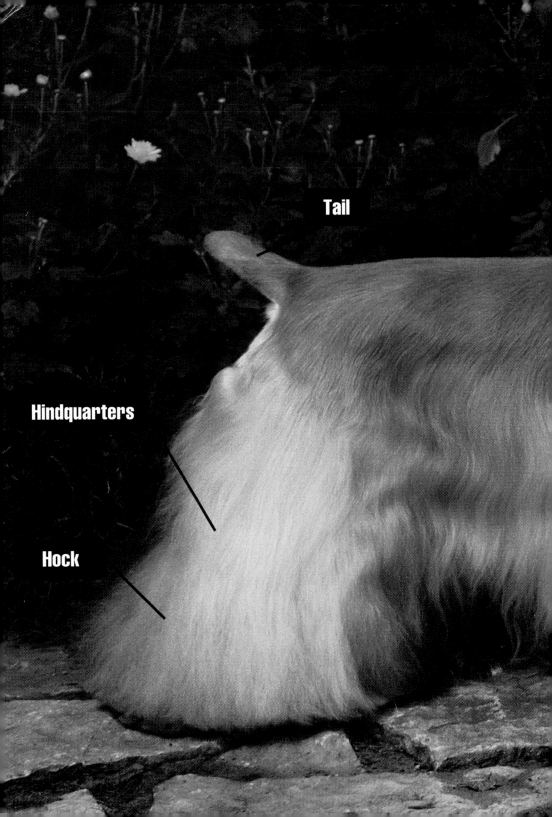

Tail

Hindquarters

Hock

Withers

Skull

Muzzle

Ears

Chest

Forequarters

Quick Facts about Dogs

Dog Terms

A male dog is called a dog. A female dog is known as a bitch. A young dog is a puppy until it is one year old. A newborn puppy is a whelp until it no longer depends on its mother's milk. A family of puppies born at one time is called a litter.

Life History

Origin: All dogs, wolves, coyotes, and dingoes descended from a single wolflike species. Dogs have been friends of humans since earliest times.

Types: There are many colors, shapes, and sizes of dogs. Full-grown dogs weigh from two pounds (one kilogram) to more than 200 pounds (90 kilograms). They are from six inches (15 centimeters) to three feet (90 centimeters) tall. They can have thick hair or almost no hair, long or short legs, and many types of ears, faces, and tails. There are about 350 different dog breeds in the world.

Reproductive life: Dogs mature at six to 18 months. Puppies are born two months after breeding. A female can have two litters per year. An average litter is three to six puppies, but litters of 15 or more are possible.

Development: Puppies are born blind and deaf. Their ears and eyes open at one to two weeks. They try to walk at about two weeks. At three weeks, their teeth begin to come in.

Life span:	Dogs are fully grown at two years. If well cared for, they may live up to 15 years.

The Dog's Super Senses

Smell:	Dogs have a sense of smell many times stronger than a human's. Dogs use their sensitive noses even more than their eyes and ears. They recognize people, animals, and objects just by smelling them. Sometimes they recognize them from long distances or for days afterward.
Hearing:	Dogs hear better than humans. Not only can dogs hear things from farther away, they can hear high-pitched sounds people cannot.
Sight:	Dogs are probably color-blind. Some scientists think dogs can see some colors. Others think dogs see everything in black and white. Dogs can see twice as wide around them as humans can because their eyes are on the sides of their heads.
Touch:	Dogs enjoy being petted more than almost any other animal. They can feel vibrations like an approaching train or an earthquake about to happen.
Taste:	Dogs do not taste much. This is partly because their sense of smell is so strong that it overpowers their taste. It is also because they swallow their food too quickly to taste it well.
Navigation:	Dogs can often find their way through crowded streets or across miles of wilderness without any guidance. This is a special dog ability that scientists do not fully understand.

Words to Know

allergy (AL-er-jee)—a sickness or a skin reaction caused by contact with something

color-blind (KUHL-ur BLINDE)—unable to see colors or the difference between colors

dingo (DING-goh)—wild Australian dog

feathering (FETH-ur-ing)—an area of a dog's coat where the hair is longer

game (GAME)—wild animals and birds that are hunted

heartworm (HART-wurm)—a tiny worm carried by mosquitoes that enters a dog's heart and slowly destroys it

litter (LIT-ur)—a family of puppies born at one time

Lyme disease (LIME duh-ZEEZ)—a serious illness that can cripple an animal or a human

microchip (MYE-kroh-chip)—a computer chip about the size of a grain of rice, implanted under the skin to identify an animal

mongrel (MUHNG-gruhl)—a dog of mixed breeding

puppy mill (PUHP-ee MIL)—a place where dogs are bred just to sell

register (REJ-uh-stur)—to record a dog's breeding records with an official club

roan (ROHN)—white mixed in with a darker color

veterinarian (vet-ur-uh-NER-ee-uhn)— a person trained and qualified to treat the sicknesses and injuries of animals

wean (WEEN)—to stop nursing or to stop depending on a mother's milk

whelp (WELP)—a puppy that is not yet weaned

withers (WITH-urs)—the tops of an animal's shoulders

To Learn More

Ackerman, Lowell. *Dr. Ackerman's Book of Cocker Spaniels*. Neptune, N.J.: T.F.H. Publications, 1996.

Alderton, **David**. *Dogs*. New York: Dorling Kindersley, 1993.

American Kennel Club. *The Complete Dog Book*. New York: Macmillan, 1992.

Brearley, Joan. *The Book of the Cocker Spaniel*. Neptune, N.J.: T.F.H. Publications, 1985.

Gannon, Robert. *English Cocker Spaniels*. Neptune, N.J.: T.F.H. Publications, 1990.

You can read articles about cocker spaniels in *AKC Gazette, Dog Fancy*, and *Dog World* magazines.

Useful Addresses

American Spaniel Club
35 Academy Road
Ho-Ho-Kus, NJ 07423

American Kennel Club
5580 Centerview Drive
Raleigh, NC 27606

Canadian Kennel Club
100-89 Skyway Avenue
Etobicoke, ON M9W 6R4
Canada

**English Cocker Spaniel Club
of America**
P.O. Box 252
Hales Corners, WI 53130

Internet Sites

allpets.com
http://www.allpets.com
Welcome to the AKC
http://www.akc.org
Breed FAQ Home Page
http://www.zmall.com/pet_talk/dog-faqs/breeds
Pet Vet: Home Page
http://www.pet-vet.com

Index